Editor Makkie Mulder

Art director Janine Couperus

Picture coordination & compilation Heleen van Gent

Assistant Ramona Floris

Coordinator line extensions Mieke Beljaarts

Text Christine van der Hoff and Loes Langendijk

Design Elise Yüksel

Photography Dennis Brandsma, Alexander van Berge,
Mirjam Bleeker, Hotze Eisma, John van Groenendaal,
Garden Picture Library, Paul Grootes, Modeste Herwig,
Eric van Lokven, Otto Polman, José van Riele, Maayke de
Ridder, Hans Zeegers.

With thanks to Bastienne van Bockel, Frans Bramlage,
Fietje Bruijn, Irene de Coninck, Nans van Dam, Angelique
Diks, Marjan Godrie, Linda van der Ham, Marita Janssen,
Mariël Kampshoff, Jet Krings, Linda Loenen, Marianne
Luning, Nina Monfils and Mette and Raven de Jonge, Naomi
Raven, Jacqueline Roeleveld, Mirjam Roskamp, Olga
Serrarens, Reini Smit, Petra de Valk, Margriet Vermee,
Monique Wiemeijer, Messrs. Maurtitz and Sneeboer.

Photographed at De Heerenhof, Stichting De Tuinen van
Mien Ruys, Heem- & Siertuin Aldenhaeve, and the gardens
of: Mirjam Bleeker, Piet Bimmel, the Drechsel family, the
Lauxtermann family, Loes Langendijk, Aride de Leeuw,
Anneke de Leeuw, the Kalkers family (design Dick Beijer),
Vera Kardaun, the Koelemeijer family, the Kruseman family,
Henriëtte van Meeuwen, Geertje Overkleeft, Elly Wagner,
Anneke van Rijs, Moniek Postma, the Weerman family
(design Henk Weijers), with thanks for their hospitality.

Illustrations Heleen van Gent

Publisher Peter Schönhuth

Printing coordination Mark van der Ham

Lithography Grafisch Service Centrum Van Tongeren

Printing Grafisch Service Centrum Van Tongeren

Published in 2001 by Conran Octopus Limited,
a part of Octopus Publishing Group
2–4 Heron Quays
London E14 4JP

www.conran-octopus.co.uk

UK edition translated by First Edition Ltd
and proofread by Libby Willis
Jacket design by Megan Smith

First published in 2000 by VT Wonen
© VNU Tijdschriften Hoofddorp 2000

British Library Cataloguing-in-Publication Data
A catalogue record for this book is available from
the British Library

ISBN 1 84091 204 9

dream gardens

find and create your perfect outdoor space

conran
OCTOPUS

CONTENTS

If you would like to be able to relax in your garden, then it should

complement your personality in the same way as your house. A garden's

style depends a great deal on how much the native greenery has been

cultivated. It is interesting to consider at this point exactly what makes

a garden a garden. Given a free rein, any 'outside space' will eventually

return to nature, and perhaps therefore cease to be a garden — if we

understand the defining feature of a garden to be that someone cares

introduction

at home in your garden

for it. On a more restrained level, a patio with stones and ornaments, a water feature and no greenery could be a very successful garden for the busy professional with little time and a hectic lifestyle. The gardens in this book are designed to fall somewhere between nature and culture: with the cottage garden and the bohemian garden nearer to nature, the classical garden somewhere in the middle and the minimalist garden closer to the abstract. The style that appeals to you most will probably reflect your personality and how you like to spend your spare time, either in relaxation and contemplation or energetically digging and weeding.

A minimalist garden starts with your ideas about the space. Do you want to make the garden seem light, or give the impression of depth or intimacy? In the same way as a room, you can achieve striking results through definition, volume and colour variations. To create a garden that derives its beauty from pure and restrained forms, you must look at your back garden with the eye of an architect in order to properly assess and balance the various spacial relationships between trees, shrubs, perennials and ground cover.

MINIMALIST

This garden is designed around rectangles and squares. Here the Indian bean trees (Catalpa bignonioides 'Nana'), with their dense crowns of heart-shaped leaves, form a dark block above the pond. The water, however still manages to catch the daylight. The path continues across a bridge of austere stepping stones.

Knocked-back colours such as white or grey are highly sensitive to the colours around them, particularly when not dominated by bright blues, yellows or reds. This is true of accessories and paving as well as the plants themselves. Their subtlety allows the leaf shapes and surface structures to play a greater role in creating depth, and gives a garden such as this one its distinct character.

colour

Choose colours to support the style of your garde
shades of grey, white and a little aubergine – four

xperiment with a simple palette of fresh green,
n flowers and red-leaved plants.

Among the simple forms of a minimalist garden, water is a magical element, symbolising free movement between rigid limits. With a pond liner and cement you can make perfect straight forms in dimensions that harmonize with your garden. The pond edge does not need to be at ground level, and a raised length of Belgian bluestone, for instance, has an understated beauty.

outline and detail

The disadvantage of looking for plants in a garden centre is that you have too little information to go on. You can only judge the plants from close up, often in their spring glory. What they will do in your garden during the course of the season is not shown and it is certainly not clear what they will look like in quantity from a distance — say, from a terrace. This is a compelling argument for visiting open gardens, and for garden books, since they can give you a wealth of information on plants.

For a minimalist garden, which looks best if there are not too many changes through the seasons, plants with mainly constant features are one answer. In other words, choose trees with a striking shape, shrubs that grow slowly, ground cover that does not flower at all (or only modestly) and perennials that take on a compact shape and do not lose that shape throughout the summer. Apart from the fact that your design stays as you first intended, this makes your garden low-maintenance, which is ideal if you lead a busy life.

Another important factor is the transition from house to garden. The path or terrace that runs up to the house wall, seen from the garden, looks best if it matches the material of the wall in style. Pay attention both to the colour and to the form and structure of the masonry. For houses with conservatories there is a design on the next page in which the paths and the width of the

pond tie in optically with the french windows. Seen from behind the pond, the lines run into each other. And in the garden on the next page large pavers help to lead the eye towards the pond. You can also reverse the principle of linking garden and house by matching the curtains or blinds in the house in colour, mood and style to the view that you have created for yourself in the garden.

Contrasts in height and depth bring a garden to life. You have several elements at your disposal for this: first the natural differences in height between plants, from ground cover to trees, which form kinds of horizontal layers. Second come all the practical extras that you can incorporate in the scheme, such as steps, fences, awnings and leafy walks. A pergola is essentially a romantic element, typical of a classical country house garden, which you would not immediately expect to find in an austere garden.

But it all depends on the choice of material and the planting. A pergola does not need to be overgrown to give an effect of space; its splendid transparent structure is even more effective without climbing plants. And a fence, which in many gardens has to be unobtrusive, can in fact play a decisive role in a 'clean' garden. A white stuccoed back wall makes a garden look wider, while a brightly coloured or darker wall brings it nearer to you and enables the shapes in the foreground to stand out.

Materials such as natural stone, gravel and zinc fit excellently into a colour palette of shades of grey; in their most basic form, particularly, they add to the character of the garden. OPPOSITE Left: steps with treads of Belgian bluestone (above) and a long narrow pond edged with the same material (below). Right: a galvanized veranda, built from industrial gratings and tubes, clad in the simplest way with sun-reflective netting. THIS PAGE Left: stones and water go well together, for example, in a basin with the water flowing or rippling over the stones (above), and a pergola as a spatial feature (below). Centre: accessories are available in matching grey. Right: a way of keeping vigorous growers in your minimalist garden – within a square frame of natural stone.

After flowering, the seed heads of a poppy (Papaver somniferum) have a dramatic and distinctive profile. On the right: fences are more noticeable in a minimalist garden than in one with denser growth, so their colour and finish plays an integral role in your design (OPPOSITE).

basic plants

A clearly defined garden starts with plants with strong shapes. Start with a sober colour palette – dark reds, whites, shades of grey and green – but also bear in mind the possibilities of plants with red foliage. OPPOSITE Left: a **chocolate cosmos** (Cosmos atrosanguineus), which truly smells of chocolate and grows up to 50cm (20in). Above right: a small **box shrub** in a deliberately selected extra-large pot. THIS PAGE Above left: the indispensable **grass**, edged by box. Above right: a **water hyacinth** (Eichhornia), a floating water plant that also looks beautiful in a large dish on the terrace. Below left: fruit trees such as **pears** and **apples** lend themselves well to strict espalier shapes, which, when mature, also form a natural sunscreen. Below right: the **Hosta sieboldiana 'Elegans'**, a shade-lover with glossy leaves and delicate lilac flowers in high summer. Apart from the basic plants on this page you will find a complete list for a minimalist garden on page 150.

THIS PAGE Above left: many species of succulents have leaves that turn lovely colours, like this **sedum**. Its flowers are secondary to its growth habit: some varieties grow in superb rosettes and are excellent as ground cover in the sun or half-shade. Above right: small **yew trees** (Taxus) in pots on either side of a teak seat. Below: the **globe thistle** (Echinops) looks as if it was designed for the minimalist garden. It grows up to 1m (3ft) high if you put it in the sun. Below left: this **hellebore** is an intriguing red-green shade. OPPOSITE Right: a young **London plane tree** (Platanus x acerifolia) that has already been trained into its final shape in the nursery. In the end it will form a dense roof of leaves, making an ideal natural parasol. Above left: an **Allium neapolitanum**, one of the many varieties of onion all of which have tall smooth stems with a compact flower head at the top. They should be planted in the autumn.

water

A minimalist garden demands elementary materials. A pond in this case consists of water that is framed with stone. The stepping stones across it play their part in reflecting their surroundings as soon as they are wet; the only green is duckweed. If you want plants and fishes in your pond, it is important to check that the water environment is suitable to keep them alive. The water must not become acid, and must also contain enough oxygen, otherwise the pond will grow thick with algae. It is important to put oxygenating plants in the water within 24 hours. As an extra you can transfer a bucket of water from a 'healthy' pond or from a stream into your pond. A pump can also provide extra oxygen to the water. Wait a few weeks before introducing your fish to the water, to ensure that any harmful chemicals from the pond liner have disappeared. It is best to plant pond plants in special aquatic compost as this does not affect the water environment.

A garden offers more than just a view, and should be more than just somewhere to stroll through. A memorable garden is interactive. Its design should tempt you to linger. Simply to sit, to smell it, to touch the roughness of a leaf or the smooth curve of a stone, to encourage a young plant to grow, or to listen, if only to the silence.

design

These umbrella plants, (Darmera peltata) stand in large square pots. The flowers of this perennial plant look like tiny umbrellas and appear before the leaves in the spring. It thrives in sun or shade and likes moist ground.

Fences, paths and patios are components that support the charisma of the garden. They can also direct your line of sight and so help to achieve visual effects. If a fence is not completely screened by plants, its height, material and finish all have a role to play in your design, as is demonstrated by the sky-blue fencing opposite. And a path not only leads from A to B, but can also describe a visual axis or emphasize a linear division. Choose practical paving material that complements your patio and masonry, and is in keeping with your plants. Combine large and small elements (like the gravel carpet around the tree trunks below), smooth with textured surfaces, and wherever possible, look for organic materials.

paving and fencing

The very best thing about a plant-free garden is that there is virtually no work to do in it. Simply relax and recline in a sun-lounger. This one, which would not look out of place on an ocean liner, is made of teak, a hard and very durable wood that can withstand winter and summer temperatures and is rainproof. It ages well, too, making it ideal for no-maintenance gardens.

sitting out

The concept of light in the garden can be interpreted broadly. Light means not only practical electric light or atmospheric candlelight, but also the daylight suffusing the garden, filtered sunlight and indirect light that is mirrored or reflected. To begin with the practical aspects: the positioning of outside lights should be part of the garden design – not only because you can assess where the wiring will have to go, but also to make sure that full justice is done to the visual elements. Apart from footpaths, terraces and your front door, you can also light up particular plants, trees and water features in various ways. Be creative and you will have two gardens in one, a day garden and a night garden. For example, a line of lights, fixed about 20cm (8in) from the ground on to a stuccoed garden wall or on both sides of steps, is both attractive and subtle. But robust spotlights for industrial use, as on the facing page, also fit into a minimalist garden and can light a patio with a grand gesture. Pay attention to the direction and placing of lights. Down-lighters suggest intimacy, while up-lighters accentuate and enlarge. A light illuminating a tree, shrub or waterfall from below emphasizes features that would otherwise be much less noticeable (such as a glossy tree trunk or the transparency of water). And if you want a garden wall to stand out, it can be illuminated strikingly with spotlights from the border, or with indirect light. You will be surprised by theatrical effects that you would never have expected.

But daylight, too, should be directed and controlled in a garden. A garden facing the sun, with light walls and paving, may be magical in the evening, but not tolerate a blazing day. The answer is screening. An awning of light sailcloth or canvas with rings to hang it from fixed hooks is, for instance, simple and effective, and easy to put up and take down as needed. A linked arrangement of London plane trees will provide a natural sun screen.

A shady garden can benefit from a clever distribution of daylight, by reflecting light off shiny garden features. A mirroring water surface; stuccoed walls; white, grey or zinc pots; and a light-coloured patio strengthen the light so that the whole garden looks lighter and larger. Planting light-coloured flowers will also contribute to this, since these are the last to stay visible in the twilight.

light

round the table

Your choice of garden furniture obviously depends a great deal on the size of your garden and the storage space available. Do you have a patio and enjoy eating out of doors, or do you have other requirements? Perhaps your ideal is reading in the shade on an relaxing seat or armchair. Or maybe you want to lie in the sun by day but sit inside in the evenings. You might also want to enjoy your garden throughout the year, with a garden hearth and barbecue arrangement where you can still be comfortable in late autumn. All these are considerations that may affect your choices.

As in the house, so in the garden **details and accessories** set the tone. In a minimalist garden, **comfortable** but **soberly** styled garden furniture is called for. You can reinforce the mood by choosing crockery, glassware, cutlery and lighting that match the ambiance. **Basic shapes** (square, circular, oval) without ornamentation, materials such as matt-glazed earthenware, zinc, glass and aluminium, and candles in grey and white look fine here. Accessories include **vases and containers** to round off the furnishing of your patio. A **simple bouquet**, composed of flowers or attractive foliage, fruit and vegetables, from your garden looks good in a pot that does not compete with the greenery. And glass containers, filled with pebbles from a garden centre and an aromatic candle, can make stable and enchanting wind-proof lights.

The term 'cottage garden' conjures up images of chickens happily scratching around and of picking your own strawberries. A cottage garden is the perfect combination of the practical and the aesthetic, one that traditionally makes optimum use of the surface area – small fruit trees, flowers for cutting and herbs are all included – making a cottage-garden arrangement an apt choice for small gardens.

COTTAGE

Ladies' mantle, poppies and harebells grow together in the cottage garden to form a cohesive mass. You will enjoy the same effect when you pick a bunch of them for your garden table.

Traditionally a cottage garden was filled with plants that offered useful elements to the gardener, so the varied play of colour emerged by chance. For today's colourful cottage garden it is a good idea to start with different shades of fruit, flowers and herbs, then combine them with the subtle hues of weathered woodwork and rustic pottery. Typical colours include blue and white, hazy mauves, and varied tints of rose-red and grey.

colour

The purplish blue of ripe plums or a red cabbag
an inviting rose gateway, the colour of your hous

e lilac of flowering mint and lavender, the pink of
l have a role to play in your cottage garden.

This is a typical cottage garden scene, a spontaneous still life with both old and new elements. A vine winds over the pergola – vines do particularly well in a sunny spot that is sheltered from the wind. They also give the advantage of a natural sun screen.

outline and detail

The English cottage garden developed centuries ago. The concept of such a charming garden, where vegetables, fruit and flowers grow all mixed up, was actually born of poverty. The original users were smallholders, and the garden was primarily a place to grow food in, not somewhere to relax – so a lawn was never part of it. Herbs were used as medicines, homegrown vegetables and fruit made up the daily menu, and anyone with any spare cash kept chickens, rabbits and bees. Everything had its use: even the walls of the houses and shed were used as supports for training fruit and other plants, and fragrant petals were scattered over the floor or sewn up in bags to scent the linen cupboard.

The materials used in the original cottage gardens mostly came from the garden itself or its immediate surroundings. The same is true of present-day cottage gardens. Fencing and entrance gates are still often made of chestnut paling or planks, and the paths are paved with pebbles. The layout of the cottage garden is uniform and usually again based on practical considerations: a straight path leading to the front door, with the traditional seat under the window, and beds on either side containing plants such as currant bushes and strawberries. The more species the better was the belief. Flowering plants and herbs that did not form large groups and that were planted individually, so that during the summer they produced an ocean of swirling colours, were characteristic of this type of garden.

In Victorian times the charm of cottage gardens was rediscovered by garden designers. Gertrude Jekyll incorporated many elements from the cottage garden into her designs and planting plans. This influence is still evident today. The nostalgic charm and intimacy of these gardens appeals to many people. Perhaps it is the unadorned simplicity of the materials, or the attraction may lie in the mixture of planting, the promise of spontaneity and surprise, the boon that you can harvest produce from your own garden and that summer mornings greet you with a heady mixture of scents.

Modern reluctance to use chemical pesticides and fertilizers suggests ecological gardening will become increasingly more important in present-day cottage gardens, so a compost heap is a must. And now that there is a growing demand for organic fruit and vegetables, just imagine how satisfying it would be if you simply had to step outside to pick something fresh to eat.

A small kitchen garden is an age-old feature of a cottage garden, with traditional crops such as radishes, onions, carrots, potatoes, beans, rhubarb and brassicas, and soft fruits such as raspberries and currants, blackberries and strawberries. The seeds can be bought from garden centres. Think ecologically and your garden will need less maintenance. Plant marigolds round the vegetable beds, to discourage aphids. Carrots and onions protect each other from insect damage as long as you mix them up (it confuses the pests and the strong smell of the onions acts as a deterrent). And you can hide a compost heap under a vegetable marrow: it will soon cover it with an umbrella of leaves and trailing vines.

When onions flower they form fragile globe-shaped umbels — eye catching, standing head and shoulders above lavender. A garden shed is for potting, pottering and paraphernalia. A few coats of paint can transform it into Snow White's cottage (OPPOSITE).

basic plants

OPPOSITE Left: the entrance to a cottage garden is often by way of a romantic **arch of roses** over a gate, for which you might choose this magnificent peach-pink **'Abraham Darby' rose**. Above right: a traditional companion of roses is **lavender**, soothing, ideal for giving a fresh scent to linen or to use in mixtures of Provençal herbs for cooking, and pretty to look at as well. THIS PAGE Above: a haze of **elder**. Below left: other culinary herbs are also attractive in a garden: **sage** (Salvia officinalis 'Tricolor'), **rosemary** (Rosmarinus), **bay** (Laurus nobilis), **basil** (Ocimum basilicum) and **thyme** (Thymus) are all easy to grow and if you let them shoot will bear lovely flowers. Species that are not hardy are best grown in pots. A good addition is **soapwort** (Saponaria officinalis), with pink flowers and leaves that when ground form a soapy lather, at one time used for washing delicate fabrics. Below right: a **raspberry bush** laden with summer berries.

Sage

Rosemary

Bay

Thyme

THIS PAGE Above: in the spring, when dark skies herald April showers, the **white blossom** of fruit trees makes a brilliant contrast. Below: pink or blue **hydrangeas** offer a bold and strong shape. The acidity of the soil determines the hue: the more acid, the more blue. OPPOSITE Right: a **grape hyacinth** (Muscari) provides a cheery splash of blue in early spring. If they are in the right place, all of these plants will spread naturally. There is a list of basic plants on page 151 to give you more ideas. Above left: finely veined petals of the **cranesbill** (Geranium). OPPOSITE Below left: the best thing about herbs and flowering perennials is that they grow up from a central point and then start spreading so that they form large clumps of colour. Here **sedum**, which does not flower until autumn, with reddish flower umbels, overlooks **catmint** (Nepeta) in the foreground.

water

A well, a pump, a small ditch: even the water in the cottage garden traditionally had a function. In a modern cottage garden the water is there for enjoyment, but (provided you do not have young children) it is actually advisable to create a pond to attract more wildlife to your garden. If you have no room for a pond, then see what can be achieved with an old tub or a water barrel sawn in half. Carefully selected pond plants, such as tall grasses, along the side of your pond should soon lead to the arrival of birds, butterflies, frogs – and perhaps even dragonflies. Then, as the sun goes down you can admire their movements while you ponder on the day's events beside the still water.

Cottage gardens were always intended to be functional and they often

owe their charm to the unplanned beauty of elements that have a

practical purpose. Such elements could be beautiful: wooden shed

doors, glass cloches to protect young vegetables, old baskets, watering

cans and enamelled pails, which on closer inspection turn out to be

perfect pots with a hole in the base. Then there are the colours of the

paint protecting wooden walls, fences and garden furniture from the

rain. Together they make up the cottage garden of your dreams.

design

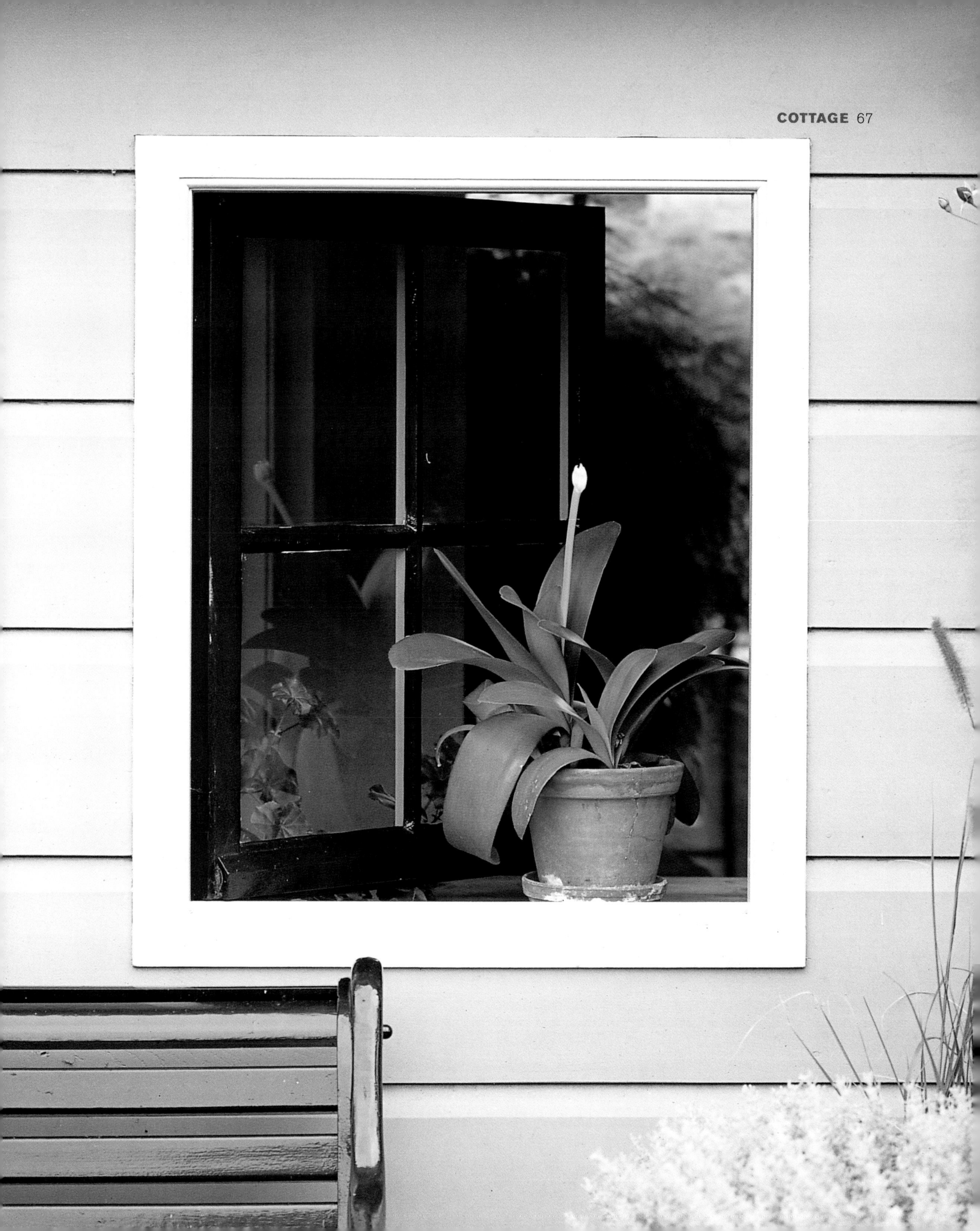

Paths are important in a cottage garden: because everything in it is picked and harvested regularly, there must be room to walk by every bed or group of plants. A hard path of clinkers or pebbles over a weedproof membrane is best – weeds will not invade it so quickly. Moreover, a hard path does not tread into the house as much as mud. Fences and gates of chestnut paling or of green-painted pine reinforce the rustic character of your garden and form a natural support for climbers such as nasturtium (Tropaeolum majus), with flowers you can use in salads and seeds to replace capers, or sweet peas (Lathyrus odoratus), which have a lovely scent. Both are annuals. There is also a perennial variety of sweet pea (Lathyrus sylvestris).

paving and fencing

Lying down, sitting or just lazing about were rare luxuries in the early cottage gardens, but times have now changed. Dreaming away happily in the garden under a parasol or an awning with a book is an almost essential garden activity. Materials and furniture that suit this type of garden are wooden seats, light-weight cane furniture or folding chairs and tables that can be taken out and put away easily.

sitting out

Introducing lighting and awnings can greatly enhance the character of a cottage garden. Your starting point should be a practical one, so that paths, gates and doors are easy to find even in the dark, and on sunny days it must be possible to protect raised areas that are exposed to the sun. But the design and colouring of a sunshade or a garden light also gives an extra injection of style to your garden. A traditional arch-shaped canopy with yellow seaside-rock stripes integrates well within the whole and sheds a warm reflection inside the house. Seen from the garden it gives the house a pleasant and familiar look that also harmonizes with the character of a cottage garden. Sunshade manufacturers will make canopies such as the one shown opposite to order, combining impregnated canvas and wood in any imaginable design.

The lighting in a cottage garden has a different function from that in a minimalist garden, where it is an additional architectural element. Here, it is a matter of illuminating the garden both sympathetically and clearly, so the distribution of the lights in the garden, and the form and material of the light fittings are particularly important. Metal, painted or weathered, is a more logical material to use than synthetics, so choose, for example, stylish traditional lanterns, such as stable lanterns, or invisible fixed lighting at ground level, which may be very modern but will not clash with the style of the garden. Round the patio, candle lanterns and oil lamps will come into their own; a welcome bonus is that they act as natural fly repellents. When seen from a distance, the twinkling lights contribute to the romantic atmosphere enfolding your house.

light

Summer, feasts can be celebrated round the table in the cottage garden, as few things are more pleasant than to savour fresh **vegetables** and **herbs** from your own garden in the open air. Dishes can be quickly garnished with a few sprigs from the border, such as **flowering herbs** or **hop vines**, or add a quickly **picked bouquet** placed in a large jug. For such an alfresco meal on the spur of the moment a large wooden table is a good base – a selection of cheerful crockery and table linen in flowery, checked or striped patterns. Choose a mixture of beautiful flower shades and they will always go together. Serve coarse farmhouse bread cut in 'doorsteps' as an appropriately rustic finishing touch.

round the table

A strong feature of the classical garden is the use of divisions such as clipped box hedges, climbing roses, symmetrical lines and decorative fountains. This style has a rich history within the gardens of country houses. What makes the classical garden special is that it is based on the control and shaping of nature, while at the same time the living and growing aspect of the planting determines its atmosphere. Classical gardens should find the most attractive balance of these qualities.

CLASSICAL

Symmetry is an important quality of a classical garden. On either side of the front door two garden urns hold Helichrysum; and in the circle of box an acacia (Robinia pseudoacacia 'Umbraculifera').

Timeless chic: the black horned violet (Viola cornuta 'Molly Sanderson').

The dominant colour in the classical garden is inevitably green, for the structure consists of bushes, shrubs and trees. Among these are flowers with strong shapes or striking blooms, for instance, red and white roses, pansies and hydrangeas, and in the spring bulbs such as tulips and irises. Leafy walks and arbours, overgrown with climbing roses or wistaria, can add a romantic touch.

colour

The amorous red of a rose, the many shades
forget-me-nots reflect the blue of the sky: th

reen in nature, the way in which wistaria and
tyle of garden demands strong colours.

outline and detail

The classical garden is based on the medieval garden, which was a sophisticated form of the monastery garden. Here monks grew herbs, such as this lavender, to cure the sick. The later country house gardens also contained flowers that were intended just for cutting and to which religious and symbolic meanings were attributed.

The classical garden with geometric lines and a symmetrical plan already existed before the Renaissance. These gardens were subdivided into equal areas along axes of sight, and planted according to rigid rules. During the Renaissance they served mainly to emphasize the honour and glory of the owner, with the implication that even mighty nature submits to civilized enlightened man. The planting was subordinate to this ethos. In the Baroque period the grand gesture gained the upper hand, so that gardens were filled in with more of a flourish. There was still a clear main axis to be seen from the house, and the garden was still subdivided in logical lines, but it had to constitute an integrated whole with the surrounding countryside, which was a new idea.

In the early nineteenth century people began to rediscover nature and attached more value to the kind of planting. England, where strict French style was followed less slavishly, became the greatest pioneer in the field of garden design. Here people thought of a new way of disciplining nature: the landscape garden, in which the natural landscape was imitated and subtly adjusted, with apparently nonchalant groups of trees on gently sloping lawns, dotted here and there with small lakes and winding streams. To give form to the then ruling cultural ideal of symmetry and organization, the art of topiary was developed to a high level. No country house could be without its topiary garden of box hedges and conifers, which adorned the prospect like green works of architecture. One particularly English invention was the Elizabethan knot garden: a garden with small hedges in various shades of green, clipped so that when seen from above they seem to form an intricate braided pattern.

Half a century later there was a reaction against these styles of garden design. The 'wild' garden, with an arbitrarily selected planting of roses, perennials and annuals all mixed up, in which there were now no restraints on nature, became the ideal. Yet the lack of structure in this scheme soon proved too impractical.

This finally resulted in the classical garden with a seemingly more natural planting. This principle is still extremely popular, because of its practicality and its fascinating and varied results. Within the classical structure profusely flowering plants are apparently given a free hand, in mixed flowerbeds or long borders. Good examples are the gardens of Sissinghurst Castle and Hidcote Manor, which attract thousands of visitors every year. In the Netherlands a good example of a classical garden design is the royal garden at Het Loo palace in Apeldoorn, created in the reign of William III and Queen Mary of England. The garden has a strict plan, and a number of special ponds and fountains, but also elements of the English landscape garden, such as disciplined lawns with enormous chestnuts and beeches. It owes part of its charm to the exotic plants from the orangery, which are put outside in the summer. June, July and August are the best months to visit it.

By introducing differences in height the garden can be made more interesting, because the whole cannot be seen at the same time. To accentuate straight lines, hedges are ideal. If you are afraid that the garden is becoming too formal, you should select many different kinds of plants, which will flower at different times, and give the garden a new look every season. For instance, wistaria (Wistaria sinensis) adorns a wall or pergola in late spring with a swirling cloak of blue flowers, before the leaves come out. Box clipped into round shapes softens the lines, and to catch the eye a plant on a single stem, such as a standard rose or a small tree, can be put in the centre. A water ornament, or a garden figure against the backdrop of a hedge, will slot perfectly into the frame of your classical garden.

The Agapanthus or African lily is a pot plant that in the nineteenth century no stylish garden could do without. From a fountain of green stems, lovely white or blue flowers shoot up high. It is not guaranteed to be winter hardy. The principles of the classical garden make an instant impact (OPPOSITE).

basic plants

OPPOSITE LEFT: with its chequerboard design the **snake's head fritillary** (Fritillaria meleagris) fits well in a classical garden. Above right: **cosmos** is very useful for filling up a bed hedged in by box, giving it a Sissinghurst effect: an abundance of flowers within a strict frame. The plants grow up to 50cm (20in) high, with feathery leaves and a florescence that seems to float above the stems. Below right: this white **peony** bud looks very like an ordinary rose. It is a beautiful basic element of purity in the classical border. THIS PAGE Above left: A **hydrangea** has the necessary nobility for a classical scheme. Above right: **wistaria** flowers in spring for three weeks, and sometimes again in late summer. Below: a **box shrub** in full glory. On the next page, and on page 150, you will find more plants for a classical garden.

THIS PAGE Above left: **Forget-me-nots** (Myosotis) form a low thick carpet of small sky-blue flowers, pretty at the edge of a border with roses, and in keeping with the medieval tradition of symbolic flowers. Above right: a decorative **David Austin rose**, **'Fisherman's friend'**, in garnet red, growing to a height of 90cm (3ft). Below: the **water lily**, queen of every pond. OPPOSITE right: in the box beds another box is clipped into a ball, surrounded by **ornamental onion** (Allium), which, with its spherical flower umbels high above the border, mirrors the clipped box. Below right: **grape hyacinths** (Muscari) come out early in spring, and are not afraid of a sudden cold snap.

water

As in the minimalist garden, the function of a water feature in the classical garden is to liven it up. It is best to keep the shape of the pond simple and severe. In the classical garden there are fewer elements along the edges of the pond to distract the attention. So no plants on the banks, because they tend to be rather obstinate and 'grassy', and would detract from the pure outline of the pond. Water plants such as lilies (Nymphaea) look splendid and attract all sorts of wildlife to the pond, from birds and butterflies to small frogs. If large-leaved water plants are not for you, then a fountain or sprinkler can add life to the surface of the water. The peaceful plash of falling water is a welcome feature in a classical garden.

A classical garden is essentially an outdoor room, which can be arranged as you would arrange any room. Closely linked hedges and clipped box give it its elegant contours. Leafy walks are most effective if they actually lead somewhere, such as to a terrace, a pond or a garden seat. Resting points for the eyes lead your gaze to them and enhance the garden: a garden figure or an old ornament at the end of a path, a fountain and pot plants from the conservatory all create an atmosphere reminiscent of French and Italian palace gardens.

design

Many classical gardens were originally courtyards and were therefore sheltered. A tall wrought-iron gate is the ideal entrance for such a garden. If you cannot have a masonry wall around it, tall hedges are a good alternative. Yew is easily clipped into formal shapes, and a beech hedge on which the brown autumn leaves stay throughout the winter is a wall in itself. Privet and hawthorn also grow very compactly if they are regularly clipped. Bricks are perfect for paving because they can be laid in different geometric patterns. A patio with stone flags or tiles of Mediterranean terracotta pavers blends well with every façade.

paving and fencing

A tiled patio is, of course, not the only place to sit in. A comfortable garden chair placed in the shade of a large shrub or tree, or on the grass itself, encourages you to stay outside all day. With folding tables it is the perfect place for an improvised picnic or evening meal. In a classical garden furniture made of traditional materials, such as wrought iron and wood, will mix well with the strong shapes of the clipped hedges.

sitting out

An arbour, a pergola covered in climbers or a romantic rose walk, such as the one opposite, covered with Rosa 'New Dawn': in the classical garden protection from the sun was often part of the design, so that when the garden was laid out they took account of the way it faced. Imagine ladies in rustling skirts, with matching parasols, walking through the garden to have tea in the arbour or on the veranda at the back of the house, and you will understand why this element was so important. But of course, a shaded walk does not have to end in an arbour or a summer house; if you have a small garden, then a bijou patio, with a hardwood Italian parasol with a cloth covering is one inventive answer. Parasols are available in square or rectangular shapes, so that they will shade the whole width of the patio. Many classical gardens have a conservatory or orangery, originally for the subtropical pot plants that stood outside in summer but had to move inside in the winter. Nowadays, many ingenious devices are available to protect them from the sun.

Lanterns, whether for candles or electric lightbulbs, are an obvious choice for lighting. From dealers in recycled building materials you can obtain attractive wall and carriage lamps with fittings that can often still be adapted to today's technical requirements. In recent years reproduction lanterns have also been designed in polished or painted steel, which look splendid set against a terrace wall or on either side of the front door. But simplified forms of fishermen's lamps, in aluminium or chrome, look good here as well. And a simple candle lantern can very easily be carried to another part of the garden.

If you have a garden with divisions, separated from each other by hedges, then it is a good idea to light each area separately. This ensures that the effect of the garden's depth is still there at night. If you light up hedges from below, for instance, with spotlights placed at a regular distance from each other along the bottom edge, you will achieve a beautiful fan-shaped theatrical effect. An ornament, statue or fountain lends itself well to subtle lighting from below. Finally, consider whether it would be possible to light up a pergola or arbour inside, so that, even at night, you will always have a covered spot to sit in.

light

For a **summer dinner party** why not transform your garden table into a festive dining table? You can very easily dress it up with a mixture of **simple accessories** (for convenience) and **decorative shapes** (where possible). **Table linen** woven with summery stripes, cream-coloured **crockery**, sturdy glasses that will not be knocked over, **cutlery** fit for any festive occasion and **large dishes** offer a warm welcome. With flaming torches and candle lanterns you can create the atmosphere of a romantic castle, adding to the style of the evening. And if it grows a little cold, put two **braziers** on either side of the table – that should keep you warm enough.

round the table

BOHEM

IAN

Would you like to mix different kinds of plants in your garden and to mix modern and classical styles? Do you dream of a patio with a fountain, or want more than anything to have a tree house and a secret vegetable patch? Maybe you hanker after a garden that is colourful and flamboyant? This chapter will have the answer: it is full of ideas to create gardens of excess and gardens of your dreams. The result is unlikely to be low-maintenance, but on the other hand you will be able to enjoy it throughout the year.

BOHEMIAN

'Bohemian' is a term used to capture the free and colourful life of Bohemian gypsies, an image that still conjures up an aura of romance as well as light-heartedness, freedom and originality. In a garden that fits this mood all your favourite colours can be included. You are at liberty to combine fuchsia pink with red, or bright blue with lime green, in any format.

colour

The festive colours of a dahlia, the warmth of
garden. The sky-blue of holiday memories, th

un-baked vegetables and fruit from your own
ight orange of a flower, dazzling and delicious...

A large expanse of grass to play in, a folding table under the tree, a meandering path and a border that holds a surprise for every day of summer: a garden can be very simple and yet perfect.

outline and detail

If you would like to give your imagination free rein, it is very important to think carefully about the layout of your garden, however contradictory that may sound. If, for example, you want many different kinds of plants in your border, or perhaps various borders or flowerbeds all different in style, then it is important to know what type of soil is in your garden: dry and sandy, wet clay, or a mixture of these. The acidity of the soil is very important, too (you can read more about this in the final section of this book). Some plants, such as bilberries, heathers and rhododendrons, will only feel happy in acid soil, whereas other plants will wither away there.

A kitchen and herb garden is an ideal component of such a garden, particularly if it faces the sun and there is a sheltered corner, for example, against a sunny wall out of the wind. If not, you might consider acquiring a greenhouse, for instance for aubergines. In such a garden you can grow all kinds of delicious vegetables, from artichokes (Cynara, also brilliant as a kind of ornamental thistle) to asparagus and courgettes, from shallots to fennel and Turkish paprikas. Put herbs such as 'Thai' basil in pots that can be taken inside on cold nights. (There are specialist nurseries that sell tropical plants.) Coriander, oregano (or marjoram), mint, borage, thyme, rosemary and sage can stand out in the full sun. Various kinds of cress are fun round the edges, including ordinary garden cress and watercress.

An exciting layout turns even a small garden into a paradise for children to play in. Winding paths, a hedge with an archway leading into a garden room, a climbing frame, a play house, or perhaps even a tree house, help to make the garden multifunctional. To embellish it you can let yourself be led by the often simple decorations from countries around the Mediterranean: the warm colours of painted walls, lanterns in the trees, weathered Spanish candle-holders on walls, or a colourfully framed Moroccan mirror — why not treat yourself? There should be water in the garden, but if you have small children who can't swim yet a safe water feature such as a mural fountain is wiser than a pond. Make sure that there are several different places where you can sit, particularly if there is something to see everywhere and the garden is full of special corners. And if there are two trees near each other, a hammock is definitely called for.

Sweet scabious
(Scabiosa atropurpurea)
has a variant popular
in flower shops, but it
is also this charming
wildflower.

OPPOSITE Left: marigolds beside a kitchen garden deter aphids and the petals can be used in salads. Above right: if you have a choice of lovely views, folding chairs and tables are convenient, as they are easy so to gather up and then reposition. Below right: dahlias come in many kinds, shades, shapes and heights. THIS PAGE Below left: a picnic table that is not in daily use is a good place to watch your homegrown cuttings mature: a kind of outdoor windowsill. Below right: hollyhocks are biennial: in the first year a tuft of leaves comes up, in the second an enormous stem full of flowers suddenly appears. In a sunny spot they easily grow up to 2m (6ft) tall.

Twining climbing plants bring romance to your bohemian garden. This passion flower (Passiflora), with its amazingly detailed flower head, will quickly climb high up against a sunny wall or fence, seeking support on its way with decorative corkscrew tendrils. A leafy walk also suits a kitchen garden; let runner beans or a vine grow over it (OPPOSITE).

Dahlias perform their colourful task splendidly both in the border and in a vase. A play house is easy to make and provides a holiday paradise that will surely guarantee unforgettable childhood memories (OPPOSITE). This one is made of pallets and a door with a diamond-shaped peephole.

basic plants

A bohemian garden is joyous, full of colour, scent and good things to eat. Opposite left: a **hollyhock** in full bloom. Above right: the splendid blue of a **Welsh poppy or** Meconopsisis. THIS PAGE Above left: a glowing ball **dahlia**. Above right: the **snowball bush** or guelder rose (Viburnum opulus), that flowers in late spring. A few sprays in a vase look stunning. Below left: juicy **blackberries**, of which more and more varieties are available without prickles, such as Rubus fruticosus 'Merton Thornfree'. Take care not to let your brambles run riot. Below right: **larkspur** (Delphinium) comes in all kinds of gorgeous colours: sky-blue, lilac and even a pale pink. There are perennial and annual varieties. Apart from these basic plants, there is another list of suggestions for planting on page 151.

THIS PAGE Above: **azaleas** have magnificent exotic flowers, underplanted here with ladies' mantle. Above centre: **spinach beet**, a vegetable fast catching up in the culinary race for fame, and a good looker in the garden, too. Above right: **hops** are fast climbers; the female plant bears these lovely bells in the autumn, and adorns a fence or garden wall delightfully. Below left: a bouquet of flowers from your own garden can have a personal charm. Below right: **peonies** (Paeonia) can, if propped up a little, have unbelievably beautiful flowers. OPPOSITE Right: an old washing basket can do good service as a weed receptacle. The sticks are for training beans or tomatoes. Below right: the delicate umbels of **cow parsley**.

water

A pond will always give an extra dimension to any garden. The water, particularly when with large-leaved water plants, will attract various amphibians and insects, such as frogs, toads and dragonflies. Birds are often to be spotted by the pond, bathing at length and drinking from the water. An advantage of a pond is that you can introduce eye-catching plants, such as water lilies and also reed mace (marvellous for children to hide behind). If your pond is at the side of the garden and your planting is fairly dense, there is a chance that you will even be visited by newts. But you can do more with water. Try letting a little cascade flow out from the garden wall into a watercourse running into a reservoir, from which the water can be pumped up again; or alternatively just put a showerhead on the garden hose for a summer shower. If you have small children unable to swim, you can allocate a spot in your garden design where the pond will go later. Meanwhile, why not make a sandpit there?

The best thing about an informal style is that you can go a long way

with ingenious solutions – ideal for anyone who has just bought a new

house so has only a limited budget left over for the garden. Painting a

wall white, or in a flower colour, has a dramatic impact. Pots, dishes

and other containers can all be different. In ethnic shops you can buy

provisions in brightly coloured tins, which make excellent cache-pots,

holding, for instance, geraniums or fuchsias. And a wind chime tinkles

merrily in the slightest breeze.

design

A wooden trellis or simple gate, overgrown with climbers, looks attractive in a romantic garden such as this one. Various kinds of ivy grow steadily and fast, as does Virginia creeper (Parthenocissus quinquefolia), and hops can cover a trellis very quickly. Wistaria (Wistaria sinensis), which twists to the left, or w. floribunda which twists to the right), like clematis and honeysuckle, is a little slower and does not usually flower in the first few seasons. For paving the patio and paths you can use anything from large pebbles and cobbles (as below) to rather cheaper wooden duckboards. Flagstones, too, are making a comeback: irregularly shaped pieces of paving, which you can turn into a crazy-paving path yourself. And perhaps you could pick up some ornaments at a flea market.

paving and fencing

Beach chairs and folding chairs are very convenient in a garden like this because you can easily tuck them under your arm and carry them to a spot in the sun, or to some pleasant cool shade. Moreover, they heighten the holiday atmosphere, and take up very little storage space. But no chair would appear out of place in this garden, from scrolled cast-iron ones to a plastic Philippe Starck design.

sitting out

If you have a garden with a number of different divisions or corners that you cannot see all at once, it is well worth installing suitable lighting throughout the garden. Do remember that this will require specially insulated cables, which must be buried at a specified depth. This will prevent you damaging one later accidentally — for instance when you are digging.

Around the terrace, alternating simple lighting ideas gives a real festive atmosphere: use a large dish with nightlights on the table, wall candle-holders or alternatively old hurricane lamps; anything you can hang in a tree, from lanterns and Christmas lights to a chandelier with candles (particularly atmospheric for a late supper under the stars).

A permanent barbecue arrangement doubles as a source of both warmth and light, and from which you can derive a great deal of pleasure all year round. At the other end of the heat scale, protection from the sun can be achieved very simply, too. The traditional white sheet kept damp with a plant spray will provide shade and a cool place on a hot day. It can be put up anywhere in the garden — maybe over a sandpit held up by a few bamboo poles stuck into the sand, or covering a balcony or terrace. The other shade-creating solution of the horizontal blind is very quick and cheap to put up with hooks in a wall and steel-wire guides — then you can draw a cloth with eyelets forwards or backwards over it. If you have a hot patio on the sunny side, build a pergola out of wood and bamboo poles, and trail a vine on the top. The leaves and branches will grow fast and grip the wood, and then, with a little luck, after a few years you will be rewarded with delicious sweet grapes.

light

The bucket-style barbecue is a brilliant invention that has magically transformed many a beach or garden picnic into a festive occasion. Charcoal goes on the middle rack, the food on the top one, and the ashes fall down below. Table decoration can be so simple (OPPOSITE). Some flowers, such as nasturtiums and marigolds and the leaves of the herb borage, can be eaten.

round the table

Flowers, bowls of **summer fruit** and a cheerful table cloth are all you need to create an atmosphere, whether you are on the terrace or picnicking on the grass. **Sunflowers** are super for interesting children in gardening: they can just put a little seed in the soil, and watch what comes up! **Purple cranesbills** are lovely for show, and you can eat the flowers of **nasturtiums**. **Crockery** does not all have to match. As long as you keep to a specific **theme**, such as decorated rims or a floral design, different purchases from antiques and secondhand shops will team together happily.

PRACTICAL ELEMENTS

You start off with a distinctive dream of your ideal garden. Then you

plan it, considering the space, the amount of light and the type of soil

at the site. The next stage is to carry out your plan and it is here that

the physical work begins. You will then become involved in the process

of sowing, transplanting, protecting and tending the plants to help them

mature. And in the summer, when your new garden is in its full glory,

you will need to develop a daily routine to keep it all in order. This

chapter will tell you how to do just that.

introduction

These garden designs are based on an average garden of approximately 6x10m (6.5x11yds)

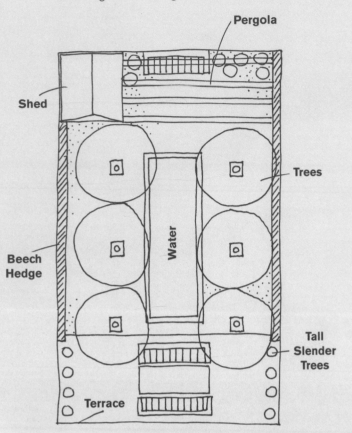

Pergola

Shed

Trees

Water

Beech Hedge

Tall Slender Trees

Terrace

MINIMALIST

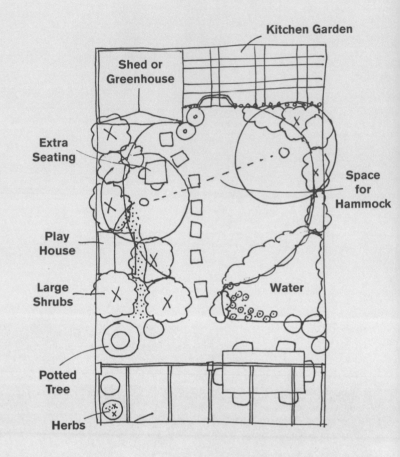

Kitchen Garden

Shed or Greenhouse

Extra Seating

Space for Hammock

Play House

Large Shrubs

Water

Potted Tree

Herbs

COTTAGE

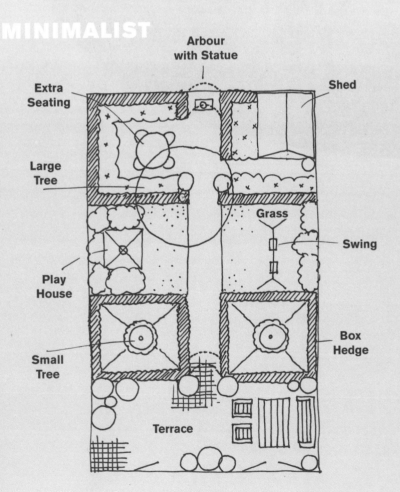

Arbour with Statue

Extra Seating

Shed

Large Tree

Grass

Swing

Play House

Small Tree

Box Hedge

Terrace

CLASSICAL

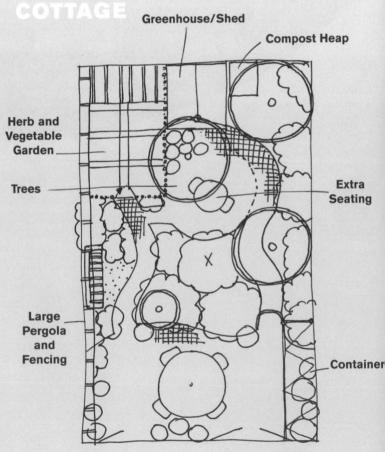

Greenhouse/Shed

Compost Heap

Herb and Vegetable Garden

Extra Seating

Trees

Large Pergola and Fencing

Container

BOHEMIAN

List of special features

This list of garden features provides a wide-ranging list of garden elements that could be integrated in a new design. If you tick those that you and your family like the sound of, then you will have a record of their special wishes for the garden that can be used as a basis for the final design.

- sandpit
- climbing frame
- tree house
- play house
- play corner
- rabbit hutch
- chicken run
- rockery
- terrace in the sun
- terrace in the shade
- (bicycle) shed
- greenhouse
- washing line
- arbour
- pergola/arbour
- statue
- ornaments
- space for logs
- container corner
- compost corner
- seat/bench
- archway into garden/entrance gate
- repotting table or corner
- conservatory
- veranda/patio

- sun dial
- lighting on terrace
- lighting on paths
- lighting in the garden
- hammock
- permanent barbecue
- fencing
- garden wall
- trellis

water features
- outside tap
- underground watering system
- rainwater butt
- fountain
- pond
- stream or water course

plants
- trees
- shrubs and bushes (flowering)
- shrubs and bushes (nonflowering)
- grass lawn
- evergreen plants
- ferns

- perennials (flowering)
- perennials (green/red foliage)
- flowering annuals
- biennials
- bulbs (spring)
- bulbs (summer)
- ground cover
- climbing plants
- conservatory plants
- water plants
- roses
- herbs
- vegetables
- fruit (trained)
- fruit (freestanding)
- flowers for cutting

paving
- decking
- tiles/flagstones
- cobbles
- shingle/shells
- grit/gravel
- brick
- grass with stepping stones

more basic plants

In a minimalist garden the planting is more or less a secondary feature. The main objective here is the arrangement. Shrubs and perennials are not mixed up but planted in large groups, preferably in blocks.

shrubs:
ivy (Hedera helix 'Arborescens')
Skimmia

bulbs:
tulip (Tulipa)
ornamental onion (Allium christophii)

conifers:
yew (Taxus)

juniper (Juniperus)
low-growing spruce (Pinus mugo)

trees:
Indian bean tree (Catalpa bignonioides 'Nana')
London plane (Platanus x acerifolia)

perennials:
heather (Erica)

Christmas rose (Helleborus)
cotton lavender (Santolina)

ornamental grass:
Miscanthus sinensis 'Malepartus'

herbs:
lavender (Lavandula)
rosemary (Rosmarinus)

MINIMALIST

In the classical garden perennials, roses and annuals can be placed in bordered beds. In contrast to the cottage garden, a single kind of planting is arranged in large groups, giving a restful and balanced picture.

roses:
classical and English roses
(David Austin roses)

perennials:
larkspur (Delphinium)
coneflower (Echinacea)
mallow (Lavatera)
lady's mantle (Alchemilla)
plantain lily (Hosta)
cranesbill (Geranium)
primula

peony (Paeonia)
Christmas rose (Helleborus)

herbs:
lavender (Lavandula)
catmint (Nepeta)

trees:
ornamental pear (Pyrus salicifolia 'Pendula')
Norway maple (Acer platanoides 'Glovosum')
magnolia

broad-leaved lime (Tilia platyphyllos)

shrubs:
hydrangea
rhododendron

hedges:
yew (Taxus)
beech (Fagus sylvatica)
privet (Ligustrum)

climbers:
passionflower (Passiflora)
clematis

CLASSIC

In the cottage garden plants can more or less do what they like. Different species are mixed up. This tapestry of plants is one of the charms of the cottage garden.

climbers:

wisteria

clematis

honeysuckle (Lonicera)

Russian vine (Poligonum aubertii)

bulbs:

daffodil (Narcissus)

grape hyacinth (Muscari)

bluebell (Hyacinthoides hispanica)

fruit:

currant, strawberry, blueberry

shrubs:

butterfly bush (Buddleia)

hydrangea

perennials:

mallow (Lavatera)

Japanese anemone (Anemone x hybrida)

sedum

lily of the valley (Convallaria)

cranesbill (Geranium)

peony (Paeonia)

Christmas rose (Helleborus)

annuals and biennials:

love-in-a-mist (Nigella)

foxglove (Digitalis)

damask violet/sweet rocket (Hesperis)

pansy (Viola)

herbs:

borage (Borago)

lavender (Lavandula)

fennel (Foeniculum)

trees:

all fruit trees, particularly species such as mulberry (Morus) and medlar (Mespilus)

all kinds of standard roses (Rosa)

COTTAGE

In this garden anything goes – as long as there is room for it.

trees:

fruit trees

wych elm (Ulmus glabra 'Camperdownii')

walnut (Juglans)

bamboo, ornamental grasses and ferns

annual herbs:

nasturtium

basil (Ocimum basilicum)

sage (Salvia)

perennials:

sweet William (Dianthus)

red-hot poker (Kniphofia)

Chinese lantern (Physalis)

Jerusalem cross (Lychnis chalcedonica)

larkspur (Delphinium)

bleeding heart (Dicentra)

butterfly bush (Buddleja)

bulbs:

snowdrops (Galanthus)

crocosmia

iris

summer bulbs:

dahlia

gladiolus

pineapple flower (Eucomis)

nerine bowdenii

vegetables:

sweetcorn, artichoke, beans, rocket, pumpkin (Cucurbita)

annuals:

zinnia

sunflower (Helianthus)

biennials:

lupin (Lupinus)

climbers:

hop (Humulus)

Virginia creeper (Parthenocissus)

BOHEMIAN

basic principles

Water, manure and air are all important. But success in the garden starts with good soil. The soil must drain well and allow the plants to get enough oxygen, develop a good root system and take in nutrients. The two extremes are sand (loose and light, but dry and poor in nutrients) and clay (rich in nutrients, but heavy and wet).

Improving the structure

There is much to be said for choosing those plants that thrive naturally in the type of soil in your garden, and yet it is possible to adapt the soil structure. Hence roses, which by nature love clay, can also be grown in sandy soil. The humus layer of soil is the top layer, rich in nutrients, which provides the roots with food. This is because useful insects and small organisms turn over the earth and pull fallen leaves below the surface, where they decay.

Using organic manures you can improve the quality of your topsoil, whether it be sand or clay. With a good layer of humus, sand is better able to hold the moisture, whereas clay is encouraged to let more water through.

Organic fertilizers consist of animal and vegetable waste (such as cattle manure, blood and bonemeal) which is scattered round the plants or mixed into the top layer of soil. This stimulates the life in the soil and feeds the plants. There is little or no nutrient value (minerals) in compost, but it will still improve the structure of the soil.

To make a humus layer yourself, you can chop the remains of dead plants into small pieces and leave them on the ground, or let fallen leaves rot. It is not necessarily a good idea to have a thorough clean-up in the garden in the autumn.

Box
Fertilizer

Cow Dung
Pellets

Rhododendron
Fertilizer

Cocoa Shells

Seed and
Cutting
Compost

Garden Turf

Compost

Grape
Fertilizer

Hydrangea
Fertilizer

Nowadays many plants have their own fertilizers, with carefully calculated dosages.

Rose
Fertilizer

Fertilized
Garden Soil

Potting Compost

Inorganic manure is artificial fertilizer. This feeds the plants faster than organic manure because it is taken up by the roots immediately, but it does not improve the structure of the soil. If you use these fertilizers, follow the directions for use carefully because they contain mineral salts that can 'burn' leaves if applied in excessively high doses.

Fertilizing: the right time

As soon as it stops freezing in early spring the soil can be fertilized. This is when plants start their growing period and will make best use of the nourishment. Roses on sandy soil need plenty of fertilizer and can be given an extra helping in early summer after their first flowering because this takes a lot of their strength. The lawn, too, which after all is kept short throughout the season and therefore has to keep on renewing its strength, can use plenty of feeding. Special lawn fertilizers are available for this, and can be used in stages. From late summer onwards you may stop fertilizing; this is when the garden starts its rest period.

SOIL TESTING

If you have questions about the soil in your garden, or if your growth results are inexplicably bad, you can have a soil test done. A sample is taken to be analysed in a laboratory. Apart from an analysis, you can also ask for expert advice on appropriate fertilizing.

Your garden centre should be able to advise you on where such tests can be carried out in your area.

IT COMES IN A PLASTIC BAG AND IT IS...

POTTING COMPOST

This is suitable when you want to grow plants in pots or containers. The mixture is relatively lightweight and contains food for about six weeks. Also, if you want to give your border plants a good start, a little potting compost can be put in the planting hole first.

SEED AND CUTTING COMPOST

A very fine light mix with little nourishment and a relatively large amount of sand, formulated for seedlings and cuttings that still have to root, and which would die if subjected to an overdose of minerals. As soon as they have more than three leaves they can go into the potting compost.

FERTILIZED GARDEN SOIL

This is suitable for filling in gaps (or tree holes) in the garden, but not good for young plants in pots or containers because it is too coarse in structure and contains too little nourishment.

ERICACEOUS COMPOST

Specially for plants that dislike lime, such as heathers, rhododendrons, azaleas and camellias.

COMPOST

Only intended to improve the structure of poor soil. You can work compost through the top layer of garden soil, or mix it with garden soil before planting anything in the open ground.

AQUATIC COMPOST

Specially prepared for planting water lilies and other water plants. There is nothing in this mix that could disturb the biological balance of a pond.

To extract composts easily from their plastic bag, there are special stainless-steel scoops with the handle reversed, so that you scoop towards yourself.

gardening tools

Gardening can be a pleasant way of spending your leisure time, allowing you to unwind in the open air. Alas, unsuitable equipment often makes it more of a chore than a pleasure. What the ideal equipment is will be affected by the size of your garden. But those listed here are a good place to start.

Garden Shears

Hedge clippers or garden shears have large handles and long blades, designed to clip a hedge well. You can also cut perennials down in the spring with them, clip box, shape conifers and tidy up grass verges.

Rake

A lawn or leaf rake is not a large investment and raking away leaves and grass cuttings keeps your lawn looking trim. These rakes are made of plastic or bamboo, but bamboo ones last only a few years. If you want one that lasts longer, invest in a leaf rake that fits on a universal handle (on which you can usually fit a hoe, too).

Trowel

This is the tool you will probably use most in practice. It will prove useful when you want to pot seedlings or small plants. When buying one, check the strength of the connection between the handle and the blade: a trowel that bends double in hard soil is useless.

Secateurs

Make a point of ensuring that your secateurs are always really sharp. There is an enormous product choice of secateurs available – there are even special secateurs for left-handed people, and smaller-sized ones for diminutive hands. If you have a garden where there is much to be pruned, it is a good idea to buy secateurs for which you can get spare parts. These are, of course, rather more expensive. They are used for pruning roses or shrubs and cutting off branches and flowers.

Watering Can

A large zinc watering can with a full load of water can be extremely heavy – this is no problem for use on the border or the lawn, but it makes it impossible to water plants in hanging baskets. So for this purpose, buy a smaller plastic watering can, preferably with a curved spout. A scale marked on the can is very helpful for applying fertilizers that have to be dissolved in the right proportions.

Small Hoe

Using a small hoe or handweeder you can remove unwanted weeds and plants that have seeded in the garden too enthusiastically. These are also useful for breaking up the ground. A long weeder is for digging up weeds with tap roots, such as dandelions.

Lawnmower

With a traditional handmower you can keep a lawn of approximately 200–300m (650–975ft) in excellent condition (and in the process keep fit as a bonus). A more expensive motormower is only necessary for a larger expanse of grass. A cylindermower will give the smoothest result; this works on the same principle as a handmower. With some rotary mowers or a strimmer the grass is cut by a nylon thread. A hovermower also achieves a satisfactory finish. The edges can be clipped with hedge clippers, with a battery-powered edge-trimmer or with an electric strimmer with an adjustable mowing head, which can be transformed into a lawn-edge trimmer.

Spade

A spade is used for cultivating and digging. A sharp-edged one can also be used to split plants. It is particularly true here that buying cheap is a false economy because only a spade made of hard rust-free metal stays sharp. When buying, take time to try the weight of the spade and choose a handle length that suits you. You should be able to lean on it while standing straight. If you are short, working with too long a spade is very tiring. Tall people are much more prone to develop an aching lower back if their spade is too short. Oiling wooden handles once a year with boiled linseed oil prolongs their life.

Saving money

Large pieces of gardening equipment, such as ladders, lawn scarifiers or earth augers (for soil sampling), are not normally used very often. Moreover, they take up a lot of space, so it is worth considering acquiring this kind of equipment jointly with neighbours or family. If that is not an option, then you can always hire large items by the day from a garden centre or plant-hire firms.

Maintenance

Tools keep in better condition if they are cleaned after use. A night spent outside in the damp air is not good for any tool. There are convenient hanging systems that can be installed in a shed so that everything can be stored in an orderly arrangement. Wiping metal tools occasionally with an oil-soaked cloth will also lengthen their life appreciably.

The kitchen garden

For a kitchen garden you need some extra equipment, such as a good hoe and a rake for the paths. If you grow tomatoes and other climbing plants, special supports along which they can grow are not an extravagant luxury. A wheelbarrow will also be used a great deal. It might be worth finding an agricultural supplier, who will sell such things as large packs of fertilizer and also young vegetables to plant out.

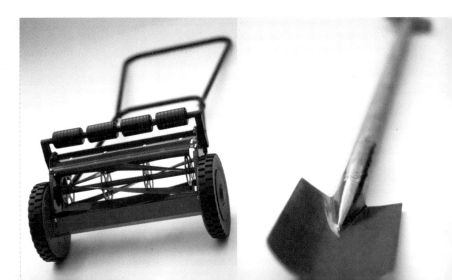

There is an abundance of garden plants for sale, but it is much more fun to propagate them yourself, particularly plants that are not readily available. Moreover, cuttings from your garden make much-appreciated presents for fellow gardeners.

Growing from seed

There are two ways of growing from seed. The first method is to use seed trays. This can be done before the beginning of spring, in a heated greenhouse or indoors. This method is only worth the effort for plants that need a long warming-up period. Species such as annual tobacco plants (Nicotiana) and cup-and-saucer vine (Cobaea) need months for the seedlings to develop from a small plant to a summer flower. If you sow them too late, their flowering season is already over before the plant is mature enough.

The second method is the simplest: scatter the seeds directly where you want them. Well-known species that can be sown in this way are annual cornflowers, marigolds, love-in-a-mist, poppies and nasturtiums. And another piece of advice: if you have children, help them to make a kitchen garden with plants that are easy to grow, such as radishes, carrots, pumpkins, cress and marigolds.

Working with seed trays

You need a seed tray with a lid, but a plastic fruit box or tray with a transparent lid from your greengrocer is also fine. Put special seed and cutting compost in the tray. Moisten the compost with a plant spray. Scatter the seeds on it as thinly as possible, but first read the instructions on the packet: some seeds need to be soaked first. Cover the seeds with a very thin layer of soil and water them with a plant spray. Now put the lid on. Then put the tray in a warm place — seeds germinate best at 21°C (70°F) — but not in bright sunlight because the shoots should not be encouraged to appear above the ground too quickly, to give the roots time to grow. Water them every day with the plant spray and when you can see a green haze of tiny leaves you can raise the lid of the tray a little further each day. When the plants have two to three leaves, they can be planted out. Take them out of the tray as gently as possible and put them in a pot with potting compost. There will be enough fertilizer in the potting compost for the next stage. Now the plants should start growing well.

From now on it is important to expose them to a lower temperature for progressively longer periods, since they will soon have to face the open air. This is called hardening off. The easiest way is to put the pots in a box and leave this outside a little longer every day. Be very careful of frost because that is fatal for most species. By late spring the risk of night frosts is usually over, so they can be put out in the open ground or in pots. Make things easy for yourself and always put a label with the plant's name in the seed tray or by a cutting. Otherwise it will be difficult for you to identify a poppy or a strawberry amid the seedlings for the first few months.

There is usually far too much seed in each packet. Perhaps you could agree with other garden enthusiasts who will sow what. Then in late spring you can swap plants.

Gardening clubs

If you have caught the gardening bug, then perhaps at some time you will decide to become a member of a gardening club. Watch out for any advertisements and announcements in special gardening magazines or local newspapers.

new plants for free: propagation

Sowing in open ground

From mid-spring onwards you can sow in open ground. The packet will tell you whether the plants should be in the sun or the shade. Rake the place where you want to sow and remove any weeds. Scatter the seed as thinly as possible or follow the instructions on the packet, and cover the seed with a thin layer of soil. Water carefully, so that the seeds are not washed away, using a watering can with a fine rose or the garden spray adjusted to its finest setting. Take care that the ground never dries out completely. If the shoots are so close that they crowd each other, they should be thinned. Be careful: poppies and other flowers with a taproot do not like being moved because they have little grip, so always sow them outside.

Cuttings

There are several ways of taking cuttings but 'summer cuttings' in particular are often successful. In late summer cut a stem about 20cm (8in) long from the plant. Cut with a sharp knife below a leaf bud and dip the cutting into rooting powder. Tap the cutting so that any surplus powder drops off. Put it in a pot with seed and cutting compost, and put a glass jamjar or special cloche over the pot. A transparent plastic bag that fits over the cutting and the pot will also do. Take care that the plastic does not touch the cutting, or first make a frame of wooden barbecue skewers round the cutting. As soon as the cutting has taken root it can be planted in a pot with some potting compost.

There are some plants, such as begonias and certain climbers, that form new 'offspring' very easily. Sometimes it is enough simply to tear off a leaf and put the torn edge with some rooting powder in the soil. Plants such as ivy, hydrangea and Virginia creeper can be propagated by letting the middle part of a branch that is still on the plant lie on the ground, and pushing it under a little. That section will spontaneously form roots and can then be cut off and planted somewhere else. This is known as layering.

Propagating perennials

In the spring and autumn you can increase your stock of perennials by dividing them, which enables them to multiply. With a sharp spade you cut off a piece of the clump and plant it in your chosen spot. With many species, such as phlox and hosta, this trick is simple and successful. However, some frost-sensitive plants like penstemon and lavatera are troublesome to help through the winter. A better idea for these is to take a small cutting that will take up very little room and can overwinter safely in a pot in a cool bedroom. In this way you will be sure of your favourite perennials the following summer.

pruning

It is good to know that many plants, shrubs and trees can be left to go their own way because they never, or hardly ever, need pruning. On the other hand, there are plants that are actually more beautiful and grow better after being pruned. In any case, you do not have to be a qualified tree surgeon to keep your garden in order. For the right approach, read on.

When to prune

It is important to know that different species of plants have to be pruned at different times. Trees, such as nut trees, birches or maples, can be pruned in the autumn and in early winter, after the sap has ceased rising. This starts up again quite early, so if they are not pruned until spring, the tree may 'bleed'. All trees can in fact be pruned in the summer because there is less risk of them bleeding once the leaves are out. However, do not remove more than a fifth of the branches, otherwise the tree will not recover properly. Willows are the exception. For shrubs an easy rule of thumb is to be guided by their flowering season. Shrubs that flower in the early part of the year should not be pruned in the spring; wait until they have finished flowering. Those that flower in summer, such as the butterfly bush, buddleia, can be cut back in the spring. They will make flower buds on the new wood that develops after they have been pruned.

What to prune with

Always use a clean and sharp instrument. Never try to cut off thick branches with shears or secateurs, but use a sharp saw, otherwise you

will, in the first place, damage the branch, and second, probably yourself, as your hand slips. When you saw off a thick branch, always ask someone to hold it, to prevent it splitting because of its weight and the wound becoming too large. A pruning cut is called a wound because the plant becomes more vulnerable to outside influences such as the weather and micro-organisms. The smaller the cut, the quicker and more easily it will repair itself. For large cuts you can apply a special wound treatment that will protect the tree.

When branches cross one another, one should be removed: choose the one that does not contribute to the rounded shape of the tree or shrub. Also, dead branches should obviously always be removed.

Hydrangeas

The buds of most species of hydrangea are formed in the previous summer, just below the flower. If you were to cut the bush back completely in the spring, you would risk having no flowers that summer. But sometimes pruning is unavoidable, for instance, if after a storm the shrub starts to droop. In this case, make sure that you cut right back all the branches that no longer grow upwards, and leave the rest. If you want to rejuvenate the shrub, cut out the oldest branches down to the ground. The hydrangea will not flower for you that summer, but it will continue to form new branches and may flower the following year.

Perennials

Withered branches of perennials can be cut down in late winter. Species such as ladies' mantle (Alchemilla) and cranesbill (Geranium) can also be cut back hard again after their first flowering. They will flower a second time. In the autumn it is best to leave perennials alone. Their dead branches protect the living part against the cold, and they often have a lovely silhouette in winter.

Roses

Most roses are pruned from early spring onwards, provided it does not freeze. Always clip above a bud facing the outside of the bush. A bud can be identified by a small stripe on the branch. Shrub roses can be cut from three to five buds above the ground. Standard roses, too, can be pruned three to five buds above the junction of the branch. For climbing roses the main stem should be left undisturbed and the side branches cut back to 2cm or 3cm (1in). Ramblers, which flower once per season and twist their way up anywhere, form their flower buds in the previous season. They mostly flower once, in early summer, so prune them after they have flowered.

Often shrubs and trees that look best in a specific shape – such as round, umbrella-shaped or espaliered – have their own specific time for pruning. When you acquire them ask when and how they should be pruned. It is a great shame if these often expensive trees lose their shape through an untimely intervention.

Hedges

Hedges can be pruned from late spring onwards. Choose a cloudy day for this, so that the sun does not shine too fiercely on the pruning cuts. Make sure in any case that the hedge has had its first clipping by midsummer's day. After that date it gets a new spurt of growth. You can give it a second clipping in late summer. The hedge will not put on new growth again that year, and it will stay pruned throughout the winter. Make sure that the hedge is clipped by early autumn to mid-autumn, before the first night frosts set in.

pests

In every garden things happen that drive the gardener to despair: snails eating all the young seedlings in one night, promising roses that just will not come up to scratch or weeds taking over in the border. Fortunately, for most of these there is a solution without having to resort to poison.

Before the advent of chemical pesticides and herbicides, people on the whole managed to keep their gardens looking beautiful. Often nature solves the problem, with or without a little encouragement. Basically, this means planting with nature in mind. If a plant is in soil in which it thrives, and in a suitable position (enough light, as much wind as it can stand), it does not struggle against the nature around it but is in harmony with it. Therefore it will be less susceptible to diseases and damage by insects. Always start by reading the information on the plant label before you buy a plant and, when designing your garden, take account of what the plants will need and the possibilities in your garden.

All kinds of creatures

Aphids, which beset the young leaves of roses in the spring, will often take to their heels after a good spurt of water. If that does not help, you can spray them with a product based on organic fatty acids. Slugs and snails are a much bigger and frequently occurring problem. Try in the first instance to catch as many as possible. It is best to do this at night – if you shine a torch on the damaged plants, the pests will come out. If you do not feel like hunting at dead of night, place plastic beakers with beer in them in the earth round the plant. The slugs and snails are lured by the smell, fall into the beer and immediately

succumb to the alcohol. Eggshells around the plant can help, too, because they form an impregnable barricade against slugs and snails. The disadvantage is that you have to look at a border full of eggshells. The good news is that much work is being done on environmentally friendly slug and snail killers. There is already a product that fights slugs biologically; ask about it at your garden centre. Lily beetles are orange beetles found mainly on lilies and fritillaries, and are easy to identify by their bright colour. When you pick them off, put your other hand below the insect, otherwise it will drop off and escape.

Birds eat many insects, including harmful ones and slugs and snails, particularly in the spring, when their eggs have just hatched and they can feed them to their young. Attract birds to your garden by putting out food and water for them in the winter and hang up nesting boxes that will encourage them to settle permanently.

Weeds

There is no garden in which weeding can be avoided: you have to do it from time to time. It only becomes a nuisance when the weeds win over the intentional planting. Ground elder and couch grass are real pests, but nettles and dandelions can be hard to get rid of, too. The disadvantage of most weedkillers is that they are not selective so can damage and destroy plants near the weed as well.

Ground elder and couch grass have an extensive horizontal root system that propagates itself invisibly. And, worse still, every separate piece of the plant can grow and put out roots. With a hoe you run the risk of simply spreading the roots. There is only one way to remove them: bit by bit using your hands. You will recognize ground elder

by its little tufts of green with seven lancet-shaped leaflets growing out of the centre. Couch grass looks like tough grass. Pay particular attention to fences because weeds such as these often move happily from the next-door garden into yours. Nettles are best pulled out wearing gloves; you can remove the long roots of dandelions with a weed spike.

Moss on the lawn

Moss on the lawn may be the result of a lack of feeding or of a certain level of acidity in the soil. Lawns that are in shade for a large part of the day can also have trouble with moss. You can try aerating the grass, and spreading lime, which influences the acidity level, and fertilizing at the right time should in the long run make the moss disappear. Actually, moss is not considered undesirable by everybody: in classical Japanese gardens some species of moss even play an important role as 'velvet' ground cover. If you have a shady garden, that may not be such a bad idea.

Doubtful cases

Some plants are pretty as a picture, but are highly invasive: they grow so strongly, or seed themselves about so lavishly, that they crowd out other plants. A respectable plant encyclopaedia will usually mention this characteristic. Often the plants you are given when you are just starting a garden are such invaders. Experienced gardeners obviously have plenty of these plants to spare, and give them to you as a friendly gesture. Thank them politely, but beware of the violet (Viola labradorica), the bugle (Ajuga), the bell flowers Campanula glomenata and C. rapunculus, the plume poppy (Macleaya), self-heal (Prunella), soapwort (Saponaria) and some golden rod (Solidagos). You should turn down any offers of spring balsam. Ferns, bamboo and grasses can all prove very invasive as well.

pots and containers

The increasing interest in gardening has resulted in pots and containers on patios and balconies being nowadays filled with many different plants. In the past they were mainly annuals, which provided colour in summer, but now there is something to look at all the year round.

The golden rule, of course, is that you must choose your plants and pots with great care, according to how much room you have. First of all, the colour and the form of the pots is more noticeable in a small area than when they are in a large garden and merge into their surroundings: they contribute to the effect of the plants you put in them and your enjoyment of the result. You can, if you want to, paint terracotta pots with latex paint in a colour that either matches or contrasts with the flowers.

Secondly, the size and shape are important. Round pots take up more valuable space than square or rectangular ones because they cannot be put so close beside or behind each other. This is particularly important on a small patio or a narrow balcony with not much room to play with. If you choose pots of different heights, you can on a relatively small floor area create an ascending 'border' of flowering plants, providing strong visual interest.

If you plant or sow anything other than annuals, you must also take account of the way their roots grow. Some plants have a rootball that fans out sideways, while other roots go down. A clematis, for instance, can flourish famously on a sunny balcony and wind itself all along the railing, but it needs a tall wide pot, and something to keep the sun off its stem because it thrives better with its feet cool. Heathers and lavender, on the other hand, feel at home in a low container or trough.

Finally, it is worth bearing in mind that a group of plants in pots is more effective if you vary the height of the foliage. If you plan to sow annuals in seed trays in the house, when buying the seed think not only of the colour but also of the expected height of the flowers and the time of flowering. Not every plant has to have its own pot, and you can put a low plant at the foot of a tall one. With just a little ingenuity you can provide yourself with a changing background of colour and scent the whole summer long.

Planting

Earthenware absorbs a lot of moisture. Before planting, put a dry pot in a bucket of water for an hour or two, to prevent it drawing too much moisture away from the new soil and roots.

The most important thing to remember for all plants in pots is to make sure that when you water them, or it rains, the water can drain away underneath. If you are planting straight into an ornamental or terracotta pot, make sure there is a drainage hole in it. If not, you can make one or more holes with a fine masonry drill. To prevent these holes getting clogged up with earth, lay potsherds over them. Then put in a generous quantity of potting compost. Tap the plant out of the garden centre's pot or, if it has stuck fast, stand it in a pail of tepid water first. Check whether the roots look healthy and cut off any dead ends. Put the rootball on the soil and see if the bottom of the plant above it is at the right height. If necessary, add more soil below because plants set too deep tend to waste all their energy in forming new roots, instead of leaves and flowers. Next fill the pot

with soil to just below the rim. If you fill it right up to the top, the soil will wash out of the pot when you water it.

There is a wide range of special potting composts available.

When winter comes

Terracotta pots can easily be cracked by frost. The soil in the pot expands with the frost and puts pressure on the inside. To prevent this you can put the plant in a plastic pot first. Those from a garden centre are ideal. Then put the plastic pot inside an ornamental one (with a drainage hole). You can store terracotta pots that are not being used in winter by turning them upside down. Then they cannot hold water, and will freeze less quickly. Of course, they can also be cleaned and put in a shed, if you have one, which saves work in the spring, too. You can in fact buy frostproof containers now, but they are usually rather more expensive than ordinary ones.

Evergreens are available ready clipped into handsome shapes such as pyramids, globes and cubes. For a striking effect put a globe-shaped one in a square container or a cube in a round pot.

The heat of summer

On a balcony or terrace facing the sun the mercury can easily run up to 45°C (113°F) in summer. A plant in a pot can then dry out in a single day, even if you have watered it that morning. The solution is to put a water tray under it and give it a little too much water. The excess water will run into the tray, and the plant can make use of it in the course of the day.

If you also put some white marble chippings on the soil, much of the heat of the sun will be reflected instead of being absorbed by the soil.

Do you often go away for the weekend? There are automatic watering systems for pots and containers, some of which can be connected to a timer device or a computer.

Many container plants originally came from hot regions and cannot stand temperatures below 5°C (41°F). Try not to give these plants water that is too cold. Fill the watering cans the day before, so that the water can warm up.

Pots, containers and hanging baskets that are out of reach can be watered with a special spray lance that simply clips on **to your garden hose. A lightweight plastic watering can with a curved spout makes a good alternative**

Feeding

Plants in pots must be fertilized in the summer. Potting compost contains enough food for about the first six weeks. After that you can water the plants from time to time with fertilizer dissolved in the water. There are also coated fertilizer pellets that only have to be given once per season. These fertilizer pellets are active over a long time and release their nutrients gradually to the plant.

legal aspects

Sometimes questions arise in gardening about what is and what is not allowed. So here are answers to some of the most frequently asked questions about rights, fences and sheds.

How tall are trees allowed to be on property boundaries?

The legal rule on the maximum height of fences and walls between two gardens is that these may not be higher than 2m (6½ft), unless you have agreed otherwise with your neighbour. For trees the rule is that they may only be planted on property boundaries by mutual agreement. From that moment they are common property and both neighbours are responsible for their height. Always take the trouble to record such agreements in writing, to consult if an argument should arise later.

Can trees and shrubs stand exactly on the property boundary?

Trees, shrubs and hedges may be planted within an agreed distance of the boundary between two properties. In many cases the planting of trees as a property boundary is subject to local government regulations, so check with your local body. There are no restrictions on hedges or shrubs.

Are you allowed to plant tall trees at the angle of a corner garden?

Sometimes shrubs and trees can prevent a good view at street corners. If there is any question of traffic safety, the issue may turn upon an interpretation of local regulations; in that case you may, for example, be forced to clip a hedge. Your local council should be able to give you full guidance on such matters.

What are easements?

Easements mean that someone has acquired the right to make use of your land in some specific way. A right of way is a frequently occurring form of easement. Your neighbours may, for example, have the right to pass through your garden to reach their own. Whenever you buy a house, always ask the estate agent if there any easements on the garden. This will be recorded in legal documents. The right remains in effect when you sell the house.

If I move house, can I take my favourite plants with me?

You can take plants with you, but only if you have agreed this beforehand with the buyer. The agreement should be added as an appendix to the sale contract. In many countries plants are deemed to be part of the house, hence the law regards them as real estate; as in the kitchen, everything 'fixed by root or nail' is thus part of the building.

Can large trees be felled?

For felling a tree, even one in your own garden, there are legal rules to abide by. These are usually laid down in the local environmental plan or in a special felling ordinance. You may apply to the council to obtain the necessary permission to fell. Some councils even demand felling permission for removing conifers.

Are there any rules about building a summer house?

Yes, but they vary with the local authority, so enquire at the town hall first. Are you obliged to obtain permission or just to report it? This depends on the place and the size of the structure. If you need permission, you will need a building licence. If you have to report it, you must submit plans and wait for their approval before you start building. You should have a decision on a building licence within 13 weeks, and for approval of plans within five weeks. Only permitted buildings, which sometimes may not be more than 1m (3ft) high, can be erected without approval.

Who owns the apples on any overhanging tree branches?

You may ask your neighbour to cut off any branches that overhang the boundary of the garden. If he or she does not do so, you may cut them off yourself, even if there are apples on them, but you must give prior notification. If you do not find the branches a problem you are in any case entitled to keep any apples that happen to drop into your garden.

May I go into my neighbour's garden for the maintenance of my house?

Sometimes you have to: you may, for instance, have to put a ladder or scaffolding in your neighbour's garden for essential maintenance or building work. Your neighbour is obliged to allow that. But there are some conditions. You must inform your neighbour in good time, and the use of his or her land must be restricted to the minimum. If any damage is done, you must compensate him or her accordingly, and you are under an obligation to take account of your neighbour's wishes.

Where exactly does the boundary of my garden run?

This is recorded at the land registry, but in practice it is sometimes vague and inconclusive. Your local authority can carry out a new survey of your property for you if necessary, but there will usually be a charge for this service. For some countries details of the land registry may be found on the Internet.

water and electricity

You have to supply water to your garden and to plants in containers, especially in periods of drought. There are all kinds of means available for this purpose, from advanced irrigation systems to watering cans with a fine rose. Particularly when designing a new garden, it is advisable to think about an irrigation system from the start. First make a scale drawing of your garden on a scale of 1:100. Mark on it where the tap is. (Make several copies of the drawing; they will always come in handy!) Take the drawing to your supplier to discuss where the sprinkler points should be set. Several different sprinklers can be fitted to underground irrigation pipes. There is even an invisible 'pop-up' system, in which the sprinklers only come up when the tap is turned on. The supply of water can be regulated automatically with a timer device; the installation can also be controlled by computer. There are even moisture sensors that can be connected to the computer for a completely self-regulating garden. For plants in pots and containers, you could install a 'spaghetti' irrigation system: each plant is connected to a supply line and a computer makes sure that the plants get the right amount of water at the right time. On roof gardens and in places with a large number of container plants this system can save an enormous amount of time.

A water butt is still an efficient way of collecting free rainwater. The water can be drawn from it by means of a special tap.

If soil is covered, it dries out less rapidly. Ground cover, and covering bare spots of soil with cocoa shells or bark, prevent it drying out.

Garden lighting

Lighting up your garden serves several purposes. At a purely practical level, to be able to see properly on the way to, for example, your garden shed or your woodpile is a must. Secondly, with a sophisticated lighting plan you can illuminate the garden splendidly and give it more depth as well as excitement. Thirdly, apart from creating atmosphere, lights can also help to prevent burglary. An infrared sensor is used to switch the light on automatically as soon as any movement is detected in the dark.

Standard mains voltage

Connecting waterproof external sockets and strong spotlights or floodlights to the mains electricity is not a job for amateurs. A small mistake in the layout can endanger life, and the cables used must have special shielding, so leave this job to a qualified professional. In order to have electricity in the garden the cables have to be laid at a specified depth, so it is best to have this done before the garden is planted out or renovated.

Low voltage

Much of the lighting for ponds, paths and small spotlights operates on a low-voltage current. A transformer converts the mains electricity into 12 volts. The transformer is installed indoors, which you can easily do yourself. There are many systems available, and they are simple to expand.

Lights that work on solar energy are fairly simple to install.

useful addresses

If you buy gardening software, you should make sure that it was produced in your own country. Guidance given on software made abroad often will not take account of your local climate.

Internet addresses

www.edenproject.com
The Eden Project is an international visitor destination in Cornwall featuring 'the living theatre of plants and people' in three biomes.

www.english-heritage.org.uk
Government agency charged with looking after many of the UK's historic sites.

www.garden.com
Extensive American site with garden accessories to send for, and an on-line magazine.

www.gardenlinks.ndo.co.uk
Gardens to visit, names of suppliers of garden products and services, research and training establishments.

www.gardenweb.com
International website offering forums, tips, events of interest to gardeners, and listings.

www.horticulture.demon.co.uk
Horticulture for All is affiliated to the Institute of Horticulture and promotes horticulture for the handicapped.

www.kew.org.uk
Royal Botanic Gardens, Kew. Information includes what's on, location, opening times, garden features and history

www.lofa.com
The Leisure and Outdoor Furniture Association, for names of suppliers.

www.nationaltrust.org.uk
The National Trust. Includes listings of historic houses and gardens open to the public in the UK.

www.nccpg.org.uk
The National Council for the Conservation of Plants and Gardens. A charity that maintains records of rare and endangered garden plants and coordinates national plant collections.

www.nts.org.uk
The National Trust for Scotland. Includes listings of Scottish historic houses and gardens open to the public.

www.rhs.org.uk
The largest and most prestigious UK garden association, the Royal Horticultural Society. With listings of gardens open to the public.

www.which.net/gardening
Helpful advice for gardeners.

Horticultural societies

Albanian Association for Decorative Flora and Fauna
Arben Rusi
Bajram Curri 85/19
Tirana, Albania

The Australian Institute of Horticulture
15 Bowen Crescent
West Gosford, NSW 2250
Australia

Garden Club of Australia
P O Box 707
Marsfield, NSW 2122
Australia

Osterreichischen Gartenbau-Gesellschaft
1010 Wien
Parkring 12/3/1
Austria

Bahrain Garden Club
Mrs Helen Preston
P O Box 26256
Manama, Bahrain

Barbados Horticultural Society
Mrs J Robinson
Ball, Christchurch
Barbados

The Garden Club of Bermuda
P O Box Hm 1141
Hamilton Hm6X
Bermuda

Horticultural Society of Ethiopia
Elizabeth Asfaw
P O Box 600074
Addis Ababa, Ethiopia

Blomsterodlingens Vanner
Ms E Koebe
Backgarden 7
Lindvagen 30-32
02270 Esbo 27, Finland

Gibraltar Horticultural Society
J T Moncur
3B Bellevue, The Vineyards
Gibraltar

Royal Horticultural Society
80 Vincent Square
London SW1P 2PE
UK

Mediterranean Garden Society
Mr D Toms
Sparoza, Box 14,
Peania 19002, Greece

Agri-Horticultural Society of India
B N Mazumder
1 Alipore Road
Calcutta 700027, India

Royal Horticultural Society of Ireland
Swanbrook House
Bloomfield Avenue
Donnybrook, Dublin 4
Republic of Ireland

Jamaica Horticultural Society
10 Mountain View Drive
Kingston 3, Jamaica

Royal Horticultural Society
Higashi-Ikebukuro SS BLD, B1
3-20-3 Higashi-Ikebukuro
Toshima-Ku, Tokyo 170, Japan

Seibu Akagi Botanical Institute
Mr M Akabane
892 Yuhikama Miniamiakagsan
Akagi-Mura, Seta-Gun
Gunma-Ken 379-11, Japan

Kenya Horticultural Society
Mr C A Renney
P O Box 4002, Nairobi, Kenya

Malta Horticultural Society
26 Medina Road
Attard, Malta BZN03

Mauritius Horticultural Society
L M Mungur
10 King George V Avenue
Floreal, Mauritius

Royal New Zealand Institute of Horticulture
P O Box 12
Lincoln University
Canterbury, New Zealand

Lagos Horticultural Society
Mrs M V Johnson
P O Box 55067
Ikoyo, Lagos
Nigeria

Det Norske Hageselkap
Postboks 9008
Gronland 0133
Oslo, Norway

Horticultural Society of Pakistan
Mr I A Mumtaz
48C Tufail Road
Lahore, Pakistan

Doha Garden Club
Mrs K M Maciver
P O Box 16970
Doha, Qatar

Singapore Gardening Society
Mr J H Tan
65 Chulia Street
123-03 OCBC Centre
Singapore 0104

Botanical Society of South Africa
Kirstenbosch
Claremont, Cape Town 7735
Republic of South Africa

Club de Jardineria de la Costa del Sol
Apartado 29
San Pedro Alcantara
Malaga, Spain

St Lucia Horticultural Society
Dr James Fletcher
P O Box 1875
Castries, St Lucia

Verband Schweizerscher Gartnermeister (VSC)
Forschstrasse 287
CH-8029 Zurich
Switzerland

Schweizerische Gesellschaft für Gartenkultur (SGGK)
Dachsternstrasse 22
CH-8040 Zurich
Switzerland

Horticultural Society of Trinidad and Tobago
Miss Emelda Rennie
P O Box 252
Port of Spain, Trinidad

The Agricultural and Commercial Society of Zambia
Mr F M C Kapoka
Showgrounds
Great East Road
P O Box 30333, Lusaka
Republic of Zambia 10101

Bulawayo Horticultural Society
Mrs Ruth Hardman
P O Box 318, Bulawayo
Zimbabwe

UK addresses

Society of Garden Designers
14/15 Belgrave Square
London SW1X 8PS
Tel. 0207-7838-9322
For names of professional garden designers.

Hardy Plant Society
Little Orchard
Great Comberton, Pershore,
Worcestershire WR10 3DP
Tel. 01386-710317

National Society of Allotment and Leisure Gardeners
O'Dell House
Hunters Road, Corby
Northamptonshire NN17 5JE
Tel. 01536-266576

Alpine Garden Society
Avon Bank, Pershore,
Worcestershire WR10 3JP
Tel. 01386-554790

Publications

The Plant Finder published by the Royal Horticultural Society tells you where you can obtain named plants. The UK edition lists international Plant Finders.

The Yellow Book lists gardens open for charity in England and Wales. Published by the National Gardens Scheme, a charity that raises money by the opening of gardens of quality and interest to the public.